Francisco Guerrero

Three Christmas Carols
for five voices

1. Oýd, oýd una cosa
   (*O hear the news*)

2. Virgen sancta
   (*Tell us, Mary*)

3. A un niño llorando
   (*To adore a tiny infant*)

Edited with an alternative English underlay
by
Anthony G. Petti

CHESTER MUSIC

EDITORIAL NOTES

Biographical details. Increasingly recognised as one of the greatest and most versatile Spanish composers of sacred music of the Renaissance, Guerrero was born in Seville, the son of a painter, in 1527 or 1528. From his brother, Pedro, he received much of his childhood training in music, and he also had a little tuition from Morales. At the age of 14 he became a chorister at the Cathedral of Seville under Fernández de Castilleja. Three years later, in 1545, he was appointed chapelmaster at Jaen, an Andalusian town about 125 miles west of Seville. Here he at first fell under a cloud, mainly for neglecting his teaching duties, but soon proved his worth. Then, after a period as chapelmaster at Málaga, Guerrero filled sundry posts at Seville Cathedral until eventually he received the highly coveted post of chapelmaster there on the death of the extremely aged Castilleja, who had held the office for sixty years. Like many of his contemporary musicians, Guerrero was given frequent leave of absence to travel widely. He twice went to Rome, and among the other places he visited were Venice, Lisbon and the Holy Land. He died in Seville in November 1599 and was buried in the Antigua chapel of the Cathedral. Guerrero's substantial compositions include masses, motets, psalms, vespers, hymns, magnificats, a Te Deum, and the spiritual songs, of which three are printed here. An excellent survey of Guerrero and his work is to be found in R.M. Stevenson, *Spanish Cathedral music in the Golden Age* (1961).

The Carols. These three carols are contained in a collection of villanescos and spiritual songs for three, four and five voices by Guerrero, published in Venice in 1589. Despite the late date of publication, the collection was composed, according to its preface, at the beginning of Guerrero's career, and Stevenson (*op. cit.*, 219-20) suggests that nearly all the pieces were written before 1555, while Guerrero was still in his twenties. The villanesco (or villancico) was a popular religious polyphonic song in the vernacular, often performed at religious festivals. It made frequent use of popular dance rhythms, and in many cases, originally had secular lyrics, usually about the joys and sorrows of love. A number of the pieces in this collection, all settings of Castilian lyrics, are Christmas carols. The poems are simple in concept, relying for their main stylistic effects on repetition, a vigorous rhythm and a close rhyming scheme even with internal rhymes. Two relevant terms in describing them are the *copla*, a quatrain unit, and the *estrebrillo*, which is the refrain of two or three lines. The estebrillo usually forms part of the *copla*, but not in the Guerrero pieces. Like most religious poems of the Renaissance, the carols rely heavily on paradox and antithesis. Thus, in No. 1, *Oýd, oýd una cosa*, the double paradox is neatly expressed that the Creator of a virgin is born the child of that virgin. In No. 2, *Virgen sancta*, a rhetorical question poses the riddle of how the supreme Creator and King could so abase himself as to be born in a mean little manger in the insignificant town of Bethlehem. No. 3, *A un niño llorando* opens with the seeming incongruity of three kings going to visit a tiny baby crying in the cold. The situation is then clarified: this child had the power to provide kingdoms, life, glory and heaven. There is almost a humorous implication in this carol that the kings certainly know what is good for them. The musical *copla* then points a moral: by demeaning himself in being born in utter poverty, God shows us how to understand the true values in life.

The settings for these lyrics provide a good idea of the variety of mood and rhythm and general vitality of the whole collection, though they are not as harmonically adventurous as some of the other pieces. Above all, as seems always the case in Guerrero, they are perfectly married to the feeling and expression of the words but not necessarily their accentuation or stress. The three pieces also demonstrate the characteristic method of setting the *copla* for a smaller combination of voices or as a solo, as a type of contrast to the main section, which is then repeated. *Oýd, oýd*, a lively piece mainly in the Ionian mode, begins fugally in duple time with a madrigalian imitation of the town crier's "oyez", which gains force by rapid augmenting of voices and the ascending pattern of fourths. A homophonic section follows which continues in triple time, and then suddenly changes into a dotted rhythm in an almost breathless *stretto* fugue. The *copla*, for the three upper voices, delicately echoes both the musical and the poetic statements of the main section. *Virgen sancta*, though alternating between duple and triple rhythm twice in its main section (the duple for the invocation and the triple for the question), is a much more sombre and restrained piece and, with the feeling of minor tonality provided by the Aeolian mode, has a smooth mystical intensity in its expression of wonderment. The main section makes a gentle, smooth and melismatic progress, while the *copla*, for solo soprano, has a very free, syncopated rhythm and an increased pace provided by numerous halved note-values. *A un niño llorando*, in the joyous Ionian mode and in a quick triple time throughout, is a rich, colourful and vivacious piece with remarkably intricate syncopation and a great feeling for gradual climax through the final phrases of the text.

Musical sources. The carols are respectively nos. 19, 18 and 26 of *Canciones y villanescas espirituales de Francisco Guerrero . . . a tres, y a quatro y a cinco bozes. Venetia, Iago Vincentio*, 1589. The only complete set of this edition known to be extant is at the Collegio del Patriarca, Valencia. The clefs, signatures and note-values of the originals are as follows:

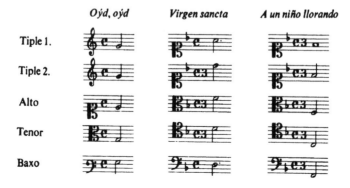

	Oýd, oýd	Virgen sancta	A un niño llorando
Tiple 1.			
Tiple 2.			
Alto			
Tenor			
Baxo			

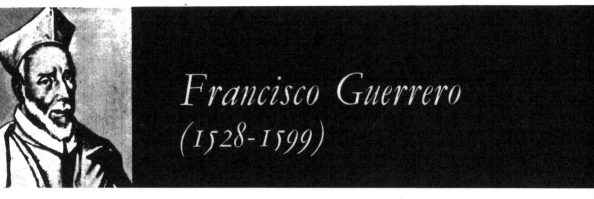

Francisco Guerrero
(1528-1599)

Three Christmas Carols
for five voices: SSATB

(Canciones y Villanescas Espirituales, 1589)

Edited
with an alternative English text
by
Anthony G. Petti

Chester Music

Editorial method, No. 1 (in *chiavi trasportati*) has been left untransposed; No. 2 (in *chiavi naturali*) has been raised one tone; and No. 3 (also in *chiavi naturali*) has been raised a major third. It is hoped that the resultant pitch will be in keeping with the timbre of the pieces, be easiest for the vocal compass, and also provide a natural transition if the pieces are performed as a group. There seemed to be no reason to apply a mechanical rule of thumb based on musicological theories, either in the transposition or in the suggestion of tempi in the reduction provided. Clearly, the C and C3 ought not to be as fast in *Virgen sancta* as they seem to be in *Oýd, oýd*. Neither has a rule been inflexibly applied that ♩·in C3 equals ♩ in C. All indications of dynamics are, of course, editorial, and have been confined to the reduction. The approximate length of performance at the tempi suggested is as follows: No. 1, 2 minutes, No. 2, 4¾ minutes; No. 3, 2½ minutes.

The text of the lyrics. The lyrics are set out in full below, divided according to their musical form and with the refrain italicised. In each case there is an additional *copla* and *da capo* verse.

No. 1. *Oýd, oýd una cosa*

Oýd, oýd una cosa
divina, graçiosa y bella:
el que crió la donzella generosa
esta noche nasçió della.

Oýd qué dichosa nueva,
qué hecho regozijado:
oy parió la Eva nueva
al hijo de Dios amado.

Sentid, sentid con cuydado
aquesta hazaña bella:
el que crió la donzella generosa
esta noche nasçió della.

Mirad qué consejo eterno,
qué grande sabiduria:
oy nasçió Dios niño tierno
en los braços de Maria.

Oýd, oýd qué alegria
divina, graçiosa y bella:
el que crió la donzella generosa,
esta noche nasçió della.

No. 2 *Virgen Sancta*

Virgen sancta, el Rey del çielo,
vuestro hijo y nuestro bien,
¿ cómo está'n un pesebruelo
de la pequeña Belén ?

El Hijo de Dios eterno
que govierna lo crïado,
está'n medio del invierno
a un pesebre reclinado.

Gran Señora, vuestro amado,
luz del çielo y nuestro bien,
cómo está'n un pesebruelo
de la pequeña Belén?

La divina hermosura
a quien cielo y tierra adora,
en un pesebruelo mora
cómo pobre crïatura.

¡ En tan baxa conpostura,
tanta alteza y nuestro bien!
¿ Cómo está'n un pesebruelo
de la pequeña Belen?

No. 3.

A un niño llorando al yelo
van tres reyes a adorar,
porqu'el niño puede dar
reynos, vida, gloria y çielo.

Nasçe con tanta baxeza,
aunqu'es poderoso rey,
porque nos da ya por ley
abatimiento y pobreza.

Por esto llorando al yelo
van tres reyes a adorar,
porqu'el niño puede dar
reynos, vida, gloria y çielo.

Alma, venid tanbién vos
a adorar tan alto nombre,
veréis qu'este niño es hombre
i mayorazgo de Dios.

I aunque pobre y pequeñuelo
le van reyes a adorar,
porqu'el niño puede dar
reynos, vida, gloria y çielo.

Notes on pronunciation. Castilian is the immediate forebear of modern Standard Spanish, and these 16th century Castilian lyrics do not differ vastly from present day usage in pronunciation. It should be noted, however, that *c*, *z* and *x* were pronounced as alveolar fricatives, the first being an unvoiced *s* (as in English "*s*ome") and the last two being a voiced *s*, or *z* (as in English "*z*ebra"). A rough guide to pronunciation is provided in the following phonetic transcription :

No. 1 *Oýd, oýd una cosa*

oˈjd oˈjd una ˈkosa diˈbina graˈsjosa‿i ˈbeʎa
ɛl ke krio la donˈzeʎa xeneˈrosa ˈesta ˈnoce naˈsjo deʎa
oˈjd ke diˈcosa ˈnweba ke ˈeco rregoziˈxaɗo
oi paˈrjo la ˈeba ˈnweba al ˈixo de ˈdjos aˈmaɗo
sɛnˈtiɗ sɛnˈtiɗ kon kwiˈɗaɗo a ˈkwesta haˈzaña ˈbeʎa

No. 2. *Virgen sancta*

ˈbirxen ˈsaŋta ɛl ˈrrɛi dɛl ˈsjelo ˈbwestro ˈixo‿i ˈnwestro bjɛn
ˈkomo es ˈtan um peseˈbrwelo de la peˈkeña beˈʎen
ɛl ˈixo de ˈdjos eˈterno ke goˈbjerna lo criˈaɗo
es ˈtan ˈmeɗjo dɛl imˈfjɛrno a‿um peˈsebre rekliˈnaɗo
gran seˈñora ˈbwestro aˈmaɗo luz dɛl ˈsjelo‿i ˈnwestro bjɛn

No. 3. *A un niño llorando*

a‿un ˈniño ʎoˈrando‿al ˈjelo ban trez ˈrrejes a‿aɗoˈrar
ˈpɔrke‿el niño pweɗe dar ˈrrɛinos ˈbiɗa ˈglorja‿i ˈsjelo
ˈnase kon ˈtanta baˈzeza a‿unkes podeˈroso rrɛi
ˈpɔrke nos da ja pɔr lɛi abatiˈmjento‿i poˈbreza
pɔr ˈesto ʎoˈrando‿al ˈjelo

For those unacquainted with the phonetic alphabet, most of the recognisable letters of the alphabet used above are pronounced roughly as in English, except that (approximately)

c   =   *ch* (as in "*ch*urch")
j   =   *y* (as in "*y*oung")
x   =   *ch* in lo*ch*

Of the other symbols, the most important to notice are

ɛ   =   *e* in "s*e*t"   ñ   =   *ni* in "opi*ni*on"
ɔ   =   *o* in "s*o*rt"   ɗ   =   *th* in "*th*en"
ʎ   =   *lli* in "bri*lli*ant"   ɟ   =   *dg* in "bri*dg*e"

The sign ˈ denotes stress, and ‿ is for elision.

It is suggested that in elision, the first vowel be passed over relatively swiftly and lightly.

THREE CHRISTMAS CAROLS

Francisco Guerrero (1528-1599)

1. Oýd, oýd, una cosa
   (O hear the news)

2

FINE

es - ta no - che nas - çió de - lla.
now be - comes her lit - tle ba - by.

-çió de - lla, nas - çió de - lla.
-tle ba - by, lit - tle ba - by.

no - che nas - çió de - lla._____
*-comes her lit - tle ba - by.*_____

no - che nas - çió de - lla.
-comes her lit - tle ba - by.

no - che nas - çió, nas - çió de - lla.
-comes her ba - by, lit - tle ba - by.

poco dim.   mf

COPLA

35

I
SOP.

O - ýd qué di - cho - sa nue - va, qué he - cho re - go - zi-
Come hear the good news we bring you, what joy - ful and hap - py

II

O - ýd qué di - cho - sa nue - va, qué he - cho____ re - go - zi - ja
Come hear the good news we bring you, what joy - ful____ and hap - py ti -

ALTO

O - ýd qué di - cho - sa nue - va, qué he - cho re - go - zi - ja
Come hear the good news we bring you, what joy - ful and hap - py ti -

Andante ♩ = c.96

mp   cresc.

[Repeat from beginning,
'Sentid,sentid', to bar 34]

8

2. Virgen sancta
(Tell us, Mary)

SOPRANO I

1. Vir - gen san - cta,   el Rey del çie - lo,
Tell   us Ma - ry,   of our Re - deem - er,
2. Gran   Se - ño - ra,   vue - stro a - ma - do,
Ho - ly mo - ther   of our dear Sa - viour,

SOPRANO II

ALTO

TENOR

BASS

Adagio ♩ = c. 70

SIMPLIFIED REDUCTION

p

5

vue - stro hi - jo y nue - stro   bien,   ¿Có - mo es - tá'n   un   pe - se -
born   your son to save - man - kind: How can   God,   who   reigns   in
luz   del cie - lo y nue - stro   bien,
Christ, the light of all   man - kind,

Andante ♩ = c. 90

cresc.   *p*

20
pe - que - ña, de la pe - que - ña Be - lén?
a man - ger, deign to lie in a man - ger?
de la pe - que - ña Be - lén?
deign to lie in a man - ger?
- ña Be - lén, de la pe - que - ña Be - len? Vir - gen san -
a man - ger, to lie in a man - ger? Tell us, Ma -
- ña Be - lén, de la pe - que - ña Be - len? Vir -
a man - ger, deign to lie in a man - ger? Tell
Vir - gen san -
Tell us, Ma -
♩=c.70
mf
meno mosso
p
25
Vir - gen san - cta, el Rey del çie - lo, el Rey del çie -
Tell us, Ma - ry, of our Re - deem - er, of our Re - deem -
Vir - gen san - cta, el Rey del çie -
Tell us, Ma - ry, of our Re - deem -
- cta, el Rey del çie - lo, vir - gen san - cta, el Rey del çie -
- ry, of our Re - deem - er, tell us, Ma - ry, of our Re - deem -
- gen san - cta, el Rey del çie - lo,
us, Ma - ry, of our Re - deem - er,
- cta, el Rey del çie - lo, vir - gen san - cta, el Rey del
- ry, of our Re - deem - er, tell us, Ma - ry, of our Re -
mp
mf

- - lo, vue - stro hi - jo y nue - stro bien,
- - er, born your son to save man - kind:
- - lo, vue - stro hi - jo y nue - stro bien, ¿có-mo es-
- - er, born your son to save man - kind: how can
- - lo, vue-stro hi - - jo y nue - stro bien, ¿có - mo es - tá'n,
- - er, born your son to save man - kind: how can God,
vue - stro hi - - jo y nue - stro bien, ¿có - mo es - tá'n un
born your son to save man - kind: how can God who
cie - lo, vue - stro hi - jo y nue - stro bien,
- deem - er, born your son to save man - kind:
Andante ♩= c.90
poco rall.
30
¿có - mo es - tá'n un pe - se - - brue - lo
how can God who reigns in splen - dour
- tá'n un pe - se - brue - lo, có - mo es -
God, who reigns in splen - dour, how can
¿có - mo es - tá'n un pe - se -
how can God who reigns in
pe - se - - brue - lo, ¿có - mo es - tá'n un
reigns in splen - dour, how can God, who
¿có - mo es - tá'n un
how can God, who

12

35

40   FINE

-ña Be - lén, de la pe - que - ña Be - lén?
a man - ger, deign to lie in a man - ger?

de la pe - que - ña Be - lén?
deign to lie in a man - ger?

-que - ña Be - lén, de la pe - que - ña Be - lén?
in a man - ger, deign to lie in a man - ger?

- lén, de la pe - que - ña Be - lén?
- ger, deign to lie in a man - ger?

-ña Be - lén, de la pe - que - ña Be - lén?
a man - ger, deign to lie in a man - ger?

COPLA

[Andante con moto ♩ = c.96]
[mf]

SOP.
SOLO

El Hi - jo de Dios e - ter - no, que go - vier - na lo crï - a - do, es-
The Son of God _ e - ter - nal, Lord of all _ cre - a - tion, now

[dim. e rall.]   D.C.

-tá'n me - dio del in - vier - no a'un pe - se - bre re - cli - na - do.
hum - bly lies in a man - ger, born a child for our sal - va - tion.

[Repeat from beginning, 'Gran Señora',
to bar 42]

14

3. A un niño llorando
(To adore a tiny infant)

16

65

70

FINE

75

glo - - ria y çie - lo.
God _____ e - ter - nal.

vi - - da, glo - ria y çie - lo.
glo - - rious, God _____ e - ter - nal.

- ria y çie - - - lo. _____
e - ter - nal.

- da, glo - ria y çie - lo.
- rious, God e - ter - nal.

glo - ria y _____ çie - lo.
God e - - - ter - nal.

cresc.

rit.

f

COPLA

[Vivo ♩ = c.180]

SOP.
[SOLO]

Nas - - çe con tan - ta ba - xe - za, aun - qu'es
Christ _____ born in such hu - mi - li - ty, though he

po - de - ro - so Rey, por-que nos da ya _____ por
is a might-y King, shows us a new way _____ of

D.C.

ley a - ba - ti - mien - to y - po - bre - - za.
life: the low - li - ness of _____ a man - - ger.

[Repeat from beginning, 'Por esto llorando al yelo', to bar 78]

The Chester Books of Motets

The first sixteen volumes of this expanding series are devoted to wide range of sacred renaissance motets with Latin texts, and contain a mixture of well known and unfamiliar pieces, some of which are published here for the first time. All appear in completely new editions by Anthony G. Petti.

1. The Italian School for 4 voices
2. The English School for 4 voices
3. The Spanish School for 4 voices
4. The German School for 4 voices
5. The Flemish School for 4 voices
6. Christmas and Advent Motets for 4 voices
7. Motets for 3 voices
8. The French School for 4 voices
9. The English School for 5 voices
10. The Italian and Spanish Schools for 5 voices
11. The Flemish and German Schools for 5 voices
12. Christmas and Advent Motets for 5 voices
13. The English School for 6 voices
14. The Italian and Spanish Schools for 6 voices
15. The Flemish and German Schools for 6 voices
16. Christmas and Advent Motets for 6 voices

An index, complete with suggested seasonal use, covering the first sixteen books of the series, is printed in Book 16.

U.S. $7.95

ISBN-13: 978-0-7119-6710-6

Distributed By

HAL LEONARD

14013466   9 780711 967106

CHESTER MUSIC LIMITED

EXCLUSIVELY DISTRIBUTED BY

HAL•LEONARD®

Order No. CH08868